Wealth Ranking in Smallholder Communities: A field manual

Barbara E Grandin

Intermediate Technology Publications Ltd, 1988

Intermediate Technology Development Group
Myson House, Railway Terrace,
Rugby CV21 3HT, UK

ISBN 185339 005 4

© Intermediate Technology Publications, 1988

Cover photo: John Young/ITDG

Printed by Russell Press Ltd, Nottingham, England.

ACKNOWLEDGEMENTS

As this manual has been based on ten years of experience marked by much assistance and helpful advice, it is impossible to acknowledge fully all who helped; neither paper nor memory suffice. However, Frank Cancian must be given credit for first suggesting the idea of wealth ranking to a struggling student. The International Livestock Centre for Africa provided the time and means for the Maasai pastoral case study, as well as time to write the manual. John Young, under the auspices of the Intermediate Technology Development Group, willingly offered to test an earlier draft of the manual and has generously allowed the incorporation of his Meru experiences into this version. The author bears sole responsibility for the content. Finally, thanks to the unsung heroes – the farmers themselves – who have taught me to listen and learn.

B E Grandin
PO Box 30709
NAIROBI
Kenya
November 1987

CONTENTS

Foreword vi

1 Why is wealth ranking useful 1

**2 Background work needed before
wealth ranking is begun 7**

3 Initial steps in wealth ranking 11

Defining the community and boundaries 11
Local concept of wealth 12
Defining the household 12
List of household heads 14
Finding several reliable local informants 15

4 Actual informant ranking 17

Introduction 17
Card sorting 18
Obtaining information on wealth differences 19
Recording the information 20

**5 Computing the average score
and grouping 29**

6 Wealth ranking in Maasailand, Kenya ..31

Actual informant ranking 31
Computing the average score and grouping
into wealth categories 33

7 Wealth ranking in Meru District, Kenya 37

Background work 38
Location-level work during the formal study period 39
Informant wealth ranking, grouping and sampling 40

Appendix A.
Checklist for wealth ranking 43

Appendix B.
Suggested reading 46

FOREWORD

When Intermediate Technology was invited, by the Kamujine Farmers' Centre in the Diocese of Meru, Kenya, to work jointly on developing their livestock project, the question of who should benefit was raised. The resources available to answer this question were very limited and it was thus essential that the preliminary survey draw on a small sample of households, representative of different income groups in the differing agro-ecological zones.

The task of arriving at this sample was made much easier (and even enjoyable) by using the 'Wealth Ranking' technique pioneered by Barbara Grandin. What had been feared as an intrusive social science instrument turned out to be an enjoyable, participative activity in which both surveyors and informants were keen to be involved. And not only were households ranked in order of perceived wealth and status but much information was also gained, rapidly and painlessly, about the economy of the communities. After analysing the results, it was relatively straightforward to select households for the detailed survey.

Intermediate Technology is pleased to be able to publish this document and conveys its deepest gratitude to the author and the Directors General of ILCA and ILRAD, respectively her past and present employers, who have allowed her time to assist the Kamujine Farmers' Centre.

Intermediate Technology is also grateful to the Catholic Fund for Overseas Development (CAFOD) and to the Overseas Development Administration (ODA) of the British Government who have granted funds to enable Intermediate Technology to work with the Kamujine Farmers' Centre livestock programme.

Patrick Mulvany
Agricultural Adviser
Intermediate Technology Development Group
July 1988

1
WHY IS WEALTH RANKING USEFUL?

Agricultural research and development must take into account differences in wealth among farmers in order to determine priorities for research and to develop interventions and technical packages that are relevant to, and adoptable by, the majority of farmers.

Inequality of some sort exists in every human society; the degree of the inequality and the attributes upon which it is based do, however, vary. Every human society defines certain differences between its members as being of great importance and values certain characteristics above others. The most common and important inequalities are based on attributes such as religion, race, ethnic group, caste and wealth (or economic status). These apply to both family units and individuals. In addition, age and gender are individual attributes which can also form the basis of social and economic inequality.

Wealth is defined in terms of *access to* or *control over* important economic resources; it is often observed through higher levels of income (and expenditure) — but these are indications of wealth rather than themselves constituting wealth. Wealth inequality is found in virtually every human community and is among the most important characteristics that differentiate people within a community. As the nature of economic resources varies from community to community, so too will the specific defining characteristics of wealth.

Wealth status is not merely an economic attribute of a person or household; it has, particularly in smallholder communities, important social and political correlates. As Chambers (1983) has so well demonstrated in what he calls the 'deprivation trap', poverty usually goes hand in hand with physical weakness, vulnerability (to hunger, illness, natural disasters, exploitation, further loss of already limited resources), powerlessness and isolation (including lack of education, services, general remoteness). Wealth is the direct opposite of this, involving strength and versatility (of the person, the household, and production strategy), patronage, authority and power, and access to both local and wider resources including education (and hence job opportunities), and other services. Thus, particularly in developing countries, the wealth status of a household[1] affects almost every aspect of the life of its members. Wealth status is, of course, not the only factor that affects a family's well-being. However, other inequalities (e.g. race, caste) are easier to identify and are also often correlated with wealth status. In most communities wealth status will be the single most important determinant of producer behaviour and family well-being.

In terms of agricultural production, wealth affects such factors as the availability of labour (both family and hired), money for purchasing inputs, or for savings and investment (often in the form of livestock). The amount of cropping, type of crops grown and use of crops (home consumption versus sales) are all likely to vary with wealth status. With regard to livestock production, wealth affects numbers and species of animals owned, and often affects management strategies and use, which in turn affect

---

[1]Although this manual deals with households, in communities where men and women have different sources of wealth women can be ranked separately from men.

Why is Wealth Ranking Useful?

overall productivity. Farmers of differing wealth will have different needs and problems and varying ability to adopt proposed technologies.

In terms of basic needs and quality of life, wealth status often directly determines the quality of the family's physical life, for example housing type, access to clean water, access to medical facilities and ability to afford them, diet and workload. Educational opportunities may vary considerably. These material differences in life are likely to affect mental and spiritual well-being, including the sense of long-term security, as well as influencing the time and energy available to participate in community affairs.

Although recent research has shown that wealth differences are fundamental in smallholder communities (even where market involvement is quite limited), many research, development and extension programmes continue to assume that all farmers in an area are basically alike. By assuming all households are similar, the question of the representativeness of farmers interviewed does not arise. Plans are then made for some mythical 'average' farmer with his 'average' family, 'average' cropping pattern, and 'average' problems. Even some community self-help programmes assess needs and assume an ability to contribute based on such 'averages', thereby excluding some people from participation. Many smallholder communities have strong *ideologies* of equality which are often misinterpreted to mean that equality *actually* exists. Planning for the 'average' farmer or household might seem simpler but it is much less effective.

In some cases, development and extension activities are not even aimed at the 'average' producer or household, but are biased (perhaps unconsciously) towards richer, more 'progressive' members of the community. Numerous criticisms have been made of such efforts in terms of their biases towards (1) communities near roads, (2) friends of the chief (or extension agent), (3) progressive or educated people, (4) households headed by males — in short, the richer, more influential members of the community (see Chambers, 1983; Leonard, 1977). Unfortunately the evidence is now overwhelming that these people are not representative of the community or area as a whole. Problems or needs they identify might not be valid for other producers.

Even those programmes which are based on the realization that there are differences between households and are explicitly concerned with reaching the poor may run into difficulty in identifying them. To a large extent this is due to the difficulties of obtaining information on the wealth of smallholders (or anybody, for that matter).

People are often unwilling to provide information on their land holdings, off-farm income, livestock sales, etc. In addition, from the researcher's point of view, it would be very time consuming to survey a whole community in order to collect enough information to determine the wealth of every member. The situation is worsened by the fact that the poor usually have low levels of involvement in community affairs. Hence there is a tendency, especially at early stages of a research or development programme, for sampling to be considerably biased towards better-off households.

The concerned agent or researcher can correct these biases, and be sure that the problems of the *whole* community are being considered by (1) carefully choosing a community (or communities) to represent the area, (2) ranking all producers in that community according to wealth, and (3) ensuring that people from all wealth statuses are included in any surveys, interviews or meetings. (While doing this, he or she can also learn enough about the area to determine to what extent other differences — e.g. ethnic group, caste, age — must also be considered.)

The rest of the manual is devoted to showing how this can be done.

Wealth Ranking in Smallholder Communities

2
BACKGROUND WORK NEEDED BEFORE WEALTH RANKING IS BEGUN

This manual assumes that the reader has some familiarity with basic approaches to Farming Systems Research (FSR). A review of these can be found in various sources (see Appendix B). Although the purpose of this manual is to explain the wealth ranking technique, it is important to review briefly the background work that needs to be done before undertaking wealth ranking. If the research or development work is to be done in a single community of up to 100 households, which has already been chosen, then wealth ranking can be done immediately (skip to Chapter 4). However, in most situations, the researcher/developer has a much wider area to cover than a single community. While the wealth ranking technique ensures the representativeness of a sample chosen *within* a community, this is of little value if the community or communities chosen are themselves not representative of the wider area. This section very briefly reviews the process of choosing representative communities for wealth ranking.

Normally FSR researchers choose a 'target area' in which they decide to work; the area may be as large as a district or even a province. Once the target area is chosen the first step is to get a general sense of the ecological diversity in the area (c.f. Figure 1). This information is often available from government maps and reports. A census and other figures can provide a rough idea of the surface area, the human and if possible livestock populations, by ecological zone; this is useful for deciding how much emphasis to put in each zone.

The next step is to determine what differences there are between communities within an ecological zone. Communities may differ from neighbouring communities for a number of reasons. The main ones are likely to be: distance to towns, markets, availability of roads, existence of farmers' groups, current or past development programmes, population density, size of land holdings and

---

I Determine ecological zones in target area
- surface area
- human population
- livestock population
- natural conditions

II Within ecological zone, determine community differences
- distance to town/market
- distance to road
- farmer group/development programme
- age of settlement
- ethnic groups
- relative wealth (and why) of different communities

III Select representative communities

IV Wealth rank within community

Figure 1 Background steps for wealth ranking within a large target group

the age of the settlement (particularly if new lands have recently been opened up). In an area where different ethnic groups predominate in different villages this can clearly have tremendous effect on social structure and agricultural production. Knowledgeable people from the area including extension agents can describe differences between communities. Once the specific differences between communities have been determined, local people can be asked whether and how they coincide with overall wealth differences between communities.

On the basis of this information, and taking into account the needs and resources of the worker on the team, a number of communities in each ecological zone should be chosen for visits and exploratory study. They should represent the diversity found in the zone. In the early exploratory phase, it is better to have as many communities as can be reasonably covered. (In later phases, if there is to be more intensive and particularly on-farm research, the number may have to be reduced for logistical reasons). Later, in analysing information obtained for these communities, the researchers should keep in mind the characteristics of each community (e.g. close to a major market town) which would help to explain results found (e.g. frequency of selling milk).

Once the communities are chosen, wealth ranking can begin. Wealth ranking is a community-based activity. The households ranked should be members of the same community, whether it is defined, for example, as a village, a neighbourhood, a ward or a group ranch. They are people who live near each other, help each other, attend each others' ceremonies and so on. As a result of close interaction (and gossiping) they know each other well.

Wealth Ranking in Smallholder Communities

3
INITIAL STEPS IN WEALTH RANKING

Informant wealth ranking is based on a card-sorting technique in which the name of each household head is written on a small card and several informants, are asked to place the cards in piles according to the wealth of each household.[2] This section and the following two sections outline the various steps of wealth ranking (the steps are summarized in Appendix A, for field use). The subsequent sections give two examples in some detail. Wealth ranking requires an assistant, fluent in the local language (and preferably from the area). It also requires a few informants from each of the communities to be ranked.

Defining the community and its boundaries

With the help of a local informant a general sense of local socio-spatial organization is obtained. In most areas there are several levels of organization from smaller to larger groups, which are like a tree, with leaves, stems, branches and a trunk. Usually there are households, often residing jointly with other households in homesteads which are, in turn, grouped into neighbourhoods, wards, villages, etc. The unit chosen in any given research site will depend on the number of households it contains. As the informants must know the people well, a unit with 100 households or less is desirable. On the other hand the unit should not be

---

[2]As noted earlier men and women can be treated separately if preferred. This might be particularly useful if women have important sources of independent income. and for projects dealing with issues under female control.

too small or sampling bias may result. If the chosen community has too many households, then the next lower social unit should be chosen (e.g. a neighbourhood of a village). If there is no social unit between the community and the homesteads, an arbitrary division of the community (e.g. the north-west portion) can be made as long as it is representative of the community as a whole.

Local concept of wealth

Most languages have a clear concept of wealth. To ensure the comparability of the data obtained from various informants, as well as to ensure that households are ranked according to the criteria the researcher desires, it is important to determine the best indigenous concept to use for ranking. This should be done with the assistant and checked with the local informants. As part of choosing the local concept it is important to understand its major components (e.g. land holdings, wage employment, livestock holdings, etc.). It is also important to verify whether this concept can be applied to a household or only to individuals.

Defining the household

A household is often defined as a group of people (normally related) who live together and 'eat from the same pot'. The implication is that the members of the household share resources and the tasks of production (including agricultural production and income-generating activities) and also share in the consumption of what the household produces. It is not always easy to identify households, particularly in societies where extended families (e.g. married children staying with their parents) are common. However, through discussions with a local informant it should not be difficult to obtain a local word or phrase to describe the household and to get an idea of the variety of forms it takes in the area. The most important thing is that, whatever unit is chosen, a comprehensive list can be obtained.

The division of labour, responsibility and production within the household is an important aspect of its functioning. In some societies women have economic activities that are independent of their husbands. Even in these societies, it is usually possible to wealth rank the household as a unit. Basic information on male/female roles can be obtained from a few informants at the initial research stage; intra-household divisions can be more fully explored for households of different wealth ranks at a later stage. If the researcher is particularly interested in a topic relating exclusively to women, it is possible in some societies to wealth rank women alone rather than the household as a unit.

For most FSR endeavours, it is simpler and more useful to rank the household as a unit and later on to explore intra-household differences. This manual is based on the assumption that the household will be used; in most societies the household is named after the head, who is often a male, but may be a female. It is the name of the head which is written on the card for sorting. The ranking should ideally apply to the household as a unit. If this is not possible, it will be necessary to rank the heads of households as individuals, and later, in discussion, to explore the relationship between the wealth of the head and the wealth of the household.

List of household heads

The technique is dependent upon ranking households of a community in relationship to each other; obviously the ranking and subsequent sampling will reflect true wealth differences in the population only to the extent that all households are included. Obtaining a complete list of households heads is the most difficult aspect of wealth ranking. Sometimes tax lists, census lists or land registry lists can be used as a basis; however, these are often incomplete and must be checked with members of the community. In a sedentary system, once the boundaries of the community have been defined, it is usually easy to sit with a few people and have them mentally 'walk' through the area giving names of the households living in each place. This can then be checked independently with another person.

In pastoral areas where producers are more mobile, obtaining a complete list of households can be more difficult. However, if dry season watering sources are limited, these places might be used as the point for obtaining names of all the households which use it. If, as in Maasailand, household heads have a neighbourhood that they consider 'home', whether or not they are present, their names can be elicited from a few residents (as in a sedentary system). However, it is essential also to determine whether there are other households currently living in the neighbourhood who do not consider it their 'home'. These should be included in the wealth ranking. In one ILCA Maasai study site, covering 1,350km^2, a neighbourhood-by-neighbourhood interview elicited the names of 206 household heads who normally use the area; this was done by a single field assistant in less than a week.

Once the list of names of household heads has been checked, each name should be written on a small card (e.g. 3 in. x 5 in.); each card should be given a number for ease of reference.

Finding several reliable local informants

The informants chosen should be long-standing members of the community who are generally knowledgeable and honest. They should be ordinary farmers who represent a *cross-section* of the community. Community leaders and/or extension agents can suggest likely candidates, but are not themselves the best people to use. The informants

Initial Steps in Wealth Ranking

can help to define the community boundaries and provide names of households. As the level of agreement among informants in wealth ranking is quite high, only 3-5 informants are necessary.[3]

In most smallholder communities, people realize that there are at least temporary differences in the wealth status of members of their community. They also recognize that people of different wealth status have very different problems of production, and often a different quality of life. As the purpose of FSR is to help people identify and solve their problems, it is easy for informants to grasp the importance of having the researchers understand such wealth differences within their community. As the informants are asked only to group people, and not to provide any sensitive information (e.g. amount of land, number of cattle), unwillingness to participate is very rare. If an informant seems reluctant or ill at ease, it is best to use another one.

---

[3]Using a total of 41 informants in 12 separate surveys, the correlations of each informant with the final score averaged 0.91 (range 0.84 to 0.98) — Spearman's Rho statistic.

Wealth Ranking in Smallholder Communities

4
ACTUAL INFORMANT RANKING

It is usually faster if the card sorting is done by each informant separately. It is acceptable (and often very informative) if two or more informants prefer to sort the cards together. However the procedure takes longer and it is still important to obtain 3 independent sortings (thus requiring more informants) to lessen biases. The sorting should be done in a quiet place where there will be no interference. A table to lay the cards on is useful, but not necessary.

Introduction

Begin by explaining to the informant the nature of the research, and the value of knowing about the different problems of rich and poor producers. Use the local word for wealth; verify that it means what you think. Ask the informant to give an example or two of differences between rich and poor, (1) generally and, (2) specifically related to the purpose of the survey. Differences will be discussed in greater detail after the card sorting; at this stage the discussion is intended to ensure the informant knows the purpose of the sorting and feels at ease about it. Discuss the concept of household and be sure the informant will rank the household as a unit and not the head as an individual.

Card sorting

Explain the actual procedure to the informant. If the informant is literate, he[4] can read the cards himself; otherwise the names will be read to him. The cards should be shuffled before being given to the informant so that they are in a random order. The only exception occurs if there is uncertainty as to whether two or more people are in the same or different households. Their cards should be kept together.

In separate sessions each informant is asked to take each card and place it before him, creating a series of piles each of which is to represent households of similar wealth status. Each informant should decide the number of piles he wants to use, as long as there are at least three. (Clearly the more piles there are, the more accurate the ranking.) At any point the informant can increase the number of piles by simply inserting a card between existing piles. Most informants will use 4 to 5 piles, although others will use up to 9. If the informant is unsure about a household he can just place that card off to the side. If the informant appears to be hesitating, encourage him not to rank that card: no information is better than guesswork. Be ready to answer any questions as the informant sorts the cards.

Once the informant has finished sorting all the cards into piles, the next step is to review each pile. Explain to the informant that you want to double check the households that he has grouped together; if he feels one or more households do not fit in that group he is free to change them into another. Beginning with one end of the row of piles (either the richest or poorest), pick up a pile and read the names.

Confirm that the informant believes they are similar in wealth. Repeat this for each pile.

Occasionally, even though an informant has many piles, he might put most of the households in one pile. As a rule of thumb, no pile should have more than 40 per cent of the households. If the informant has a pile with 40 per cent or

---

[4]The masculine pronoun (he, him, himself,) is used generically throughout this book to denote both male and female.

more of the households, ask him if there are differences between those households. If there are, ask him to further subdivide that pile into two or more piles (see the Maasai example in the next chapter.

Obtaining information on wealth differences

In the process of sorting the cards and verifying the groupings, the informant will be constantly thinking about wealth differences in his community. After the sorting has been verified, it is a good time to discuss in greater detail the nature of the differences between people of different wealth ranks. Do not ask about specific households, as this might be sensitive information. The informant will still have the piles of cards in front of him as an aid to memory. Faced with the pile of cards of similar producers, it will be easy for the informant to explain more fully to the researcher what makes people in one group different from people in other groups. Usually it is easier to begin with the richest group. Point to the pile and ask what this group of farmers (pastoralists), for example, have in common, and they have that makes them rich. Repeat this for each pile. If the informant has many piles it may be helpful to remind him which pile is being discussed by reading a few names from it.

At the end of this exercise the researcher will have a very good idea of what factors define wealth differences within the community. These factors will vary considerably across communities. It is important at this stage to let the informant say what he thinks the important characteristics are.

After the informant has finished describing each of the piles in his own way, the researcher should then ask specific questions relevant to his own research interests. For example, for a livestock health programme, the informant could be asked how problems with livestock keeping differ across wealth categories and, more specifically, whether there are differences between these wealth groups in the use of veterinary drugs. This sort of information is very helpful in choosing topics for subsequent interviews. If possible, take notes while discussing these issues. This is also a good time to discuss household versus individual wealth if this has been raised earlier as an issue.

Recording the information

As soon as the informant has been thanked and left, it is important to record the information obtained, both the actual ranking (household number by pile) and any comments on individuals or groups. Figure 2 shows a sample recording sheet used in Maasailand.

Actual Informant Ranking

```
            WEALTH RANKING - Olkarkar Group Ranch
Informant. _____  Date: _____
Age: _____  Assistant: _____
Neighbourhood: _____

1.  Richest _____
    _____
2.  _____
    _____
3.  _____
    _____
4.  _____
    _____
5.  _____
    _____
6.  _____
    _____
7.  _____
    _____
8.  _____
    _____
9.  _____
    _____
10. _____
    _____
UNKNOWN: _____

Comments: _____
_____
_____
_____
_____
_____
```

Figure 2 Sample recording sheet

Wealth Ranking in Smallholder Communities

```
                    WEALTH RANKING - Olkarkar Group Ranch
    Informant: Kenedi (15A)           Date: Jan 20 1982
    Age: Ilmirishi                    Assistant: T de Thomasya
    Neighbourhood: Lesoropoyo
```

                                                                    SCORE
1. Richest 8, 9, 11 (B), 12, 14, 16, 17, 18, 21, 22, 27, 28,   ⎫ See
   30, 33 (A+B), 38, 39, 40, 41, 42, 46   ⎬ below
                                                                  ⎭ 17, 33

2. 4, 6, 10, 11 (A+C), 15(A), 19, 20, 23, 24, 25, 31,   50
   32, 36, 37, 43, 47

3. 2, 3, 5, 7, 34, 35, 48   67

4. 1, 13, 26, 27A, 28A, 45   83

5. 29   100

6.

7. ↗ 5) has no animals, works
      elsewhere. Could divide
      category 1 into 2 sub-groups

8.   by size of herd. Large: 11B, 12,
      14, 16, 18, 28, 30, 33/39 (A+B), 40, 42

9.   (score 17). Smaller: 8, 9, 11, 21, 22,
      27, 38, 41, 46 (score 33). Rank

10.   partly depends on family size; if
      small family can be 'rich' with

UNKNOWN: 44   fewer animals. Number of final piles 6.

Comments: This young informant more readily separated brothers,
but still combined sons living with their fathers
(including himself). CATEGORIES: 1) Rich have more than
enough property; can help others. 2) Have just enough; can't help others. 3) Poor, but still independent.
4) Poor and dependent on other households for assistance.

Figure 3 Completed recording sheet

Actual Informant Ranking

```
                WEALTH RANKING - Olkarkar Group Ranch
Informant: Kitikin                Date: Jan 19 1982
Age:       ILMIRISHI              Assistant: T ole Ramya
Neighbourhood: Lesuasrii
```

                                                                    SCORE
1. Richest 12, 14, 33 (A+B), 2A, 40   20

2. 8, 9, 11, 15(A), 16, 18, 21, 28, 37, 42, 46   40

3. 4, 6, 11A, 17, 19, 22, 23, 27, 30, 32, 36, 43,
   47   60

4. 7, 11C, 13, 20, 25, 26, 27A, 44, 45, 48   80

5. 1, 2, 3, 5, 29, 34   100

6.

7.

8.

9.

.0.

UNKNOWN: 10, 11B, 24, 28A, 31, 35, 38, 41

Comments: 11B not known as not sure what animals
in father's herd are his. Two extra cases
as separated 11A from 11C and 11B from 11A.

Figure 4 Completed recording sheet

WEALTH RANKING – Olkarkar Group Ranch

Informant: TIKOYI (47) Date: Jan 18, 1982

Age: Ilmirishi (26-36) Assistant: F Ole Simba

Neighbourhood: LESUKUROI

Pile		Score
1. Richest	33 (A, B), 39	11
2.	14, 16, 40	22
3.	18, 28	33
4.	12, 42	44
5.	8, 9, 11 (B), 15 (A), 21, 22, 27, 30, 36 (23), 46	56
6.	4, 6, 11A, 17, 20, 38, 43 (44), 47	67
7.	10, 11C, 19, 27A	78
8.	1, 2, 5, 7, 25, 28A, 32, 48	89
9.	3, 13, 26, 29, 34, 45	100
10.		

UNKNOWN: 24, 31, 35, 37, 41

Comments: 11A + 11C have separated from their father. Although A+C do everything together, he says he knows 11A has more animals. – Wealth (ORKASIS) is primarily based on the animals one owns. (Emaki or 'property') Wealth can change quickly during drought or misuse or just bad luck. Small stock numbers are included in figuring wealth, but they are much less important than cattle numbers. Land or business could be included, but none of these men have any.

Figure 5 Completed recording sheet

Actual Informant Ranking

```
           WEALTH RANKING - Olkarkar Group Ranch
Informant: PARMUSHO (#39)          Date: Jan 18, 1982
Age: Iseuri age-set                Assistant: F ole Simba
Neighbourhood: ORPAIRE
```

                                                                    Score

1. Richest 11(B), 12, 14, 16, 18, 21, 24 (30), 28, 33 (A,B), 39,
            40, 46   25

2. 8, 9, 11A(C), 15(A), 17, 20, 22, 23 (36), 27, 31, 37,
    41, 42, 47   50

3. 4, 6, 7, 19, 25, 27A, 32 (36), 43   75

4. 1, 2, 3, 5, 10, 13, 26, 28A, 29, 34, 44, 45, 48   100

5.

6.

7.

8.

9.

10.

UNKNOWN: 38

Comments: 11A+C are completely independent of 11+11B now, but not from each other. Brothers who have never separated and can't be ranked separately. 24+30, 23+34, 32+36. Category 4 people cannot support their families. They need help from other people. Category 3 people can just support their families. They have nothing to spare to help others. 28A was separated from his father, then lost his animals and is now largely dependent on his father.

Figure 6 Completed recording sheet

Household Number [1]	Informant Ranking Scores [2]				
	INF 1	INF 2	INF 3	INF 4	Avg. Rank Score [3]
1	83	100	89	100	93
2	67	100	89	100	89
3	67	100	100	100	92
4	50	60	67	75	63
5	67	100	89	100	89
6	50	60	67	75	63
7	67	80	89	75	78
8	33	40	56	50	45
9	33	40	56	50	45
10	50	-	78	100	76
11 (B)	17	40	56	25	35
11 A	(50)	60	67	(50)	57
11 C	(50)	80	78	(50)	65
12	17	20	44	25	27
13	83	80	100	100	91
14	17	20	22	25	21
15 (A)	50	40	56	50	49
16	17	40	22	25	26
17	33	60	67	50	53
18	17	40	33	25	29
19	50	60	78	75	66
20	50	80	67	50	62
21	33	40	56	25	39
22	33	60	56	50	50
23	50	60	(56)	(50)	54
24	50	-	-	(25)	-
25	50	80	89	75	74
26	83	80	100	100	91
27	33	60	56	50	50
27 A	83	80	78	75	79
28	17	40	33	25	29
28 A	83	-	89	100	91
29	100	100	100	100	100
30	17	60	56	(25)	40
31	50	-	-	50	50
32	50	60	89	(75)	69
33 (A+B)	17	20	11	25	18
34	67	100	100	100	92
35	67	-	-	(75)	-
36	50	60	(56)	(50)	54
37	50	40	-	50	47
38	33	-	67	100	50
39	17	20	11	25	18
40	17	20	22	25	21
41	33	-	-	50	42
42	17	40	44	50	38
43	50	60	(67)	75	63
44	-	80	(67)	100	82
45	83	40	100	100	81
46	33	40	56	25	39
47	50	60	67	50	57
48	67	80	89	100	84

1 ( ) indicates a household ranked with another. Thus 15 (A) means 15 and 15 A always ranked together.
2 ( ) means that score was joint with another household.
3 - household deleted as there are not two independent ranking scores.

Figure 7 Maasai score by Informant (1-4) and Average

Actual Informant Ranking

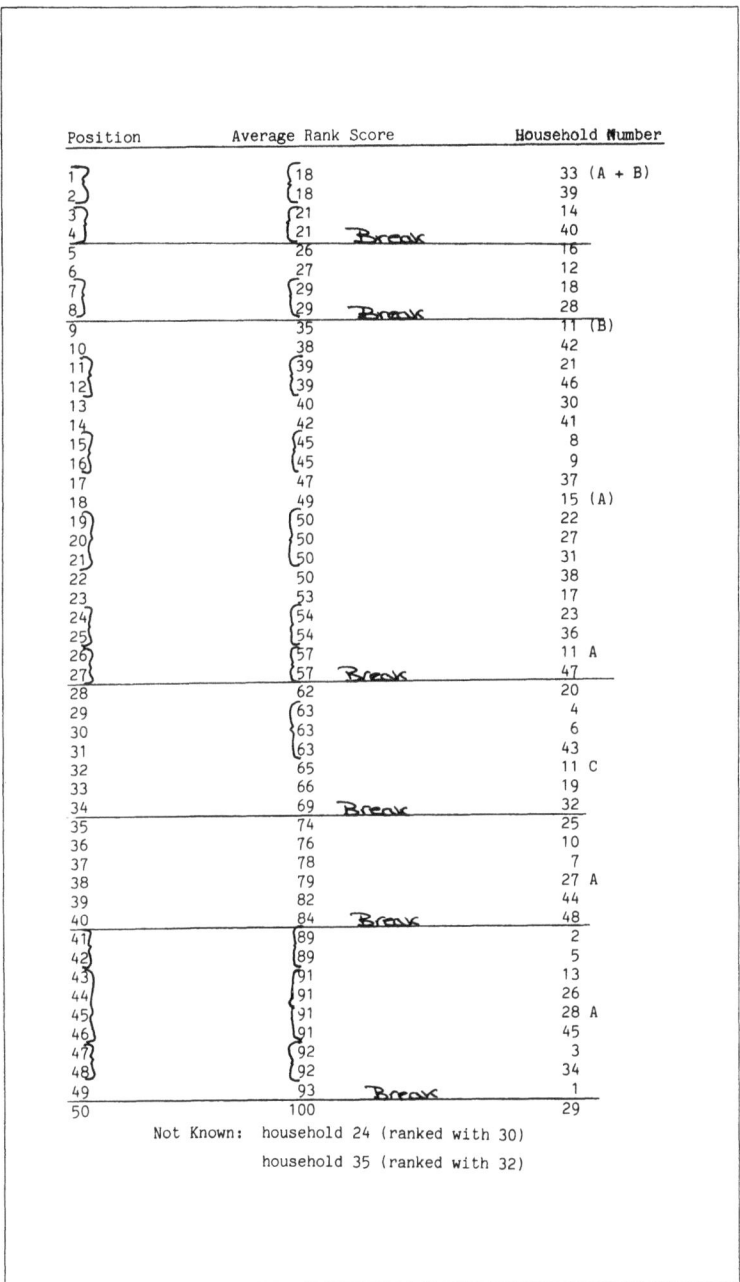

Figure 8 Rank order of the Households

Wealth Ranking in Smallholder Communities

5
COMPUTING THE AVERAGE SCORE AND GROUPING

The procedure outlined in Chapter 4 should be repeated with at least two other informants. The scores of the three (or more) informants must then be combined to obtain an average score for each household. The simplest way in which the individual informant's score can be compiled into an average score for each household is to give each household a score for each informant which is: its pile number divided by the total number of pile.[5] For ease of calculation these fractions are multiplied by 100 and rounded. If a household is in the first (richest) of six piles, its score is 1/6 times 100 which equals 17; if it is in the fifth pile, it is 5/6 times 100 which equals 84. For each household, these scores are added together, and then divided by the number of rankings available. While these calculations are done, scan the data for informant reliability. If one informant consistently disagrees with the others, try to find out why. (This has never to my knowledge occurred.) It is more likely that a few households will have scores which are highly inconsistent (i.e. ranked richest once, and poorest by another informant). If time permits, more details on these households might be obtained and be very informative.

---

[5] I am indebted to John B Raintree for suggesting this simple method, which is that used by de Walt (1979). This method was compared to a more difficult method using the arithmetic midpoint of each group as the score for the farmers in that group. In the four cases compared the correlation between the two methods (r^2) was 0.986.

Because of the way the average scores are calculated they will be distributed along a continuum ranging from a small number (for the richest households) to 100 (for households who are consistently placed in the poorest pile). The next step is to list the household numbers according to their score from the smallest number to 100, which is from richest to poorest. Next the households need to be grouped into a number of wealth strata. (To use the absolute scores obtained would not be valid but would represent a false degree of accuracy.) As a rule of thumb, the number of final groups should not be more than the average number piles used by the informants. It can be fewer, depending on the researcher's interests, but not less than three. Normally, for ease of comparison, the size of the final groups should be roughly equal. When the size of groups cannot be equal because of the clustering of scores, it is better for the middle group or groups to be larger and the extremes (richest/poorest) to be slightly smaller.

6
WEALTH RANKING IN MAASAILAND, KENYA

This section briefly describes an application of the wealth ranking technique in Kenya Maasailand done by the author for a single group ranch. The primary purpose was to test the feasibility and validity of wealth ranking for pastoral peoples. It was done in fairly early stages of the author's work in Maasailand, but after a costly complete livestock and human census had been conducted by other ILCA personnel. There was a very high correlation (0.97) between the informant ranking and a ranking of households based on livestock units held (see Grandin (1983) in Appendix B). In fact, the informant wealth ranking brought to light a number of census errors.

Actual informant ranking

First the names of each compound were obtained; there were 18. Then the name of every independent household was obtained on a compound by compound basis. Households are named after their heads who are almost always male. In this area the livestock is considered as belonging to the household head. Women do not own livestock of their own and have essentially no independent economic activity. Thus the wealth of the head of the household is defined as being the same as the wealth of the household. There was some difficulty in determining whether a household was independent or dependent on another household (e.g. a married son who had not separated from his father). In most cases young married sons living with their father were felt to be dependent; to be on the safe side they were listed separately, but given numbers related to their fathers; so if the father was Number 11 his sons would be 11A and 11B. Their cards were kept together to give the informants a chance to decide whether to rank them separately or together. There were 48 clearly independent men and nine possibly independent sons/brothers. These were fairly consistently grouped into 52 household units.

Four informants of different ages and neighbourhoods were asked separately to rank these producers. Before the actual ranking, I briefly discussed with each informant the concept for wealth (*emali*) which my Maasai assistant and I had chosen to use. We talked of the fact that different producers are of different wealth status and have different problems. All informants (rich and poorer) heartily agreed, and offered examples (food shortages, labour shortages, etc.).

The name of each household had been written on a separate, numbered index card. The assistant read the name of each producer, and the informant took the card and placed it in the appropriate pile. Each informant decided on the number of piles he wanted to use. If he hesitated, the assistant enquired as to the problem. Sometimes, the problem was that the producer fell between two existing piles of cards; we suggested adding a new pile. Sometimes the informant did not know the producer well enough and the card was put to the side. Sometimes, the producer was felt to not be independent and thus difficult to rank; at this time the particulars of that producer's situation were noted. After all the cards were sorted, the assistant took each pile and read the names to give the informant a chance to review the groups he had compiled. Two informants moved a few cards from one pile to another; one informant decided the producers in one pile were too different and he split that pile into two piles. One informant (Kenedi) originally had 20 cards in the rich pile; he was asked if this could be split further and he did so readily. Figures 3, 4, 5 and 6 show the actual recording sheets for the four informants, as well as initial comments made (detailed comments on wealth differences were recorded elsewhere and are not shown). The number of piles used ranged from four to nine with a mean of six. The number of producers an informant could not rank ranged from one to eight.

Computing the average score and grouping into wealth categories

Figure 7 shows the listing of the informants' scores and the calculations of the average score for the Maasai sample. Two decisions needed to be made before the score could be calculated: how to treat missing data, and how to treat cases where two producers were sometimes ranked as a single unit. It was decided that two independent ranks were required for a case to be valid. When two producers were ranked together all the time (e.g. 11 and 11B) they were treated as a single household. If they were sometimes ranked together and sometimes separately (e.g. 23 and 36 were ranked separately twice and together twice) it was decided to rank them separately as long as there were two independent ranks. When they were ranked together, they were both given the same score for that informant. This is noted by the brackets for ease of counting valid ranks. Households 24 and 35 were excluded for lack of information, leaving 50 valid cases. If more time had been available, more information could have been gathered on these households. As they were both joint ranked with other producers, information on them would have been obtained if the latter had been selected for interview.

As the mean score is computed it is essential to scan each household to check for consistency of scores; there should not be too great a difference between the informants' scores for the same household. This also picks up the inevitable errors in transcription. On the whole the scores are very consistent. The largest discrepancy appears to occur in household 10 which was put in pile three of six by informant one, but in pile four of four by informant four. In looking at the raw data however, the discrepancy is not so large as at first appears, as informant one has only a total of 14 households in the bottom three piles.

The next task is to decide how to group the households. The number of groups depends partly on the interests and resources of the researcher. However, for most projects, three groups (rich, average, poor) are sufficient. In any case, the number of groups should not exceed the mean of the number of piles used by the informants (six in this case). To have more groups than the informants would be false accuracy. Ideally each group will have about the same number of households, and about the same interval range of scores (ie the difference between the highest and lowest scores). If the interval range of one group is much larger (two or more times) than the other groups, this may mean that the group is very heterogeneous. Either the group should be subdivided or more information should be acquired about the higher and lower households in the group.

In Maasailand, after the average score was calculated, the households were put in order from the lowest to the highest. The easiest way to do this is to write the average score boldly on the index cards, and then sort the cards from the lowest score number to the highest. Then write them out as in Figure 8. As the average rank score is written down, it will be clear that some households share the same score and sometimes there is a large gap (natural break) between the scores of one household and the household following it. The actual dividing points are a compromise between having roughly equal size groupings and using natural breaks in the average rank scores. In this example, if three groups are desired each should contain about 16 to 17 cases, so cut-offs are needed near positions 17 and 34. Scanning the scores we see the large natural breaks, as shown in Table 1.

After position	Size of break	No. of households included	Interval
4	5	4	18-21
8	7	4	26-29
27	5	19	35-37
34	5	7	62-69
40	5	6	74-84
49	7	9	89-93
End	End	1	1-100

Table 1 Natural breaks in the Maasai sample

Looking from the top there is no large natural break near position 17, but there is a break after position 34. The following 16 households (positions 35-50) would be defined as the poor group. As there is no large break near position 17, a more arbitrary break is needed. Looking back at Figure 8, position 17 is preceded and followed by a break of two. There are no larger natural breaks nearby. Breaking after position 16 seems preferable as it leads to 3 groups of 16, 18 and 16 households respectively.

Next the interval ranges are checked. As the scores range from 18 to 100, a difference of 82, the approximate interval range of each category should be: 82 divided by 3, or 27. The final Maasai intervals were 18-45 (range of 27), 42-69 (range of 22), and 74-100 (range of 26). As the ranges are very similar, the dividing points are confirmed. Once the groupings are made, sampling for interviewing can be done, if desired.

Although random sampling is preferred, opportunistic sampling would be much easier and faster, and as long as it is proportional to the number of households in the wealth group, would still ensure representativeness. In choosing opportunistically within a wealth category, try to get households which cover the interval range. For example if three groups were used in the Maasai work, the richest group would have 16 households with an average score range of 18 to 45. If interviews were to be done with three households, they should be spread across the range; for example, it would not be recommended to interview households 33, 40 and 12, (with scores of 18, 21, and 27), while ignoring the households with slightly lower scores. It might be useful to interview either 33 or 39 to understand the circumstances of the richest household in the area, but this should then be counterbalanced by interviewing one household in the middle (e.g. 12) and one of the households with a lower score (e.g. 41).

7
WEALTH RANKING IN MERU DISTRICT, KENYA

Wealth ranking was used as one part of a feasibility study conducted for a farmer training centre[6] which was considering the desirability of initiating livestock courses for local farmers. The study was (1) to determine the need for livestock courses and their possible content and (2) to provide baseline data for later project evaluation.

The time, money and manpower available for the feasibility study were limited. The early stages of the study covered background work (as described in Section 2). The service area of the centre covers five very different agro-ecological zones (AEZ) from semi-arid plains to well watered mountain slopes. The type of agricultural and livestock production systems vary tremendously across these zones. It was decided to conduct formal interviews with a number of representative farmers in the area. Once representative communities were chosen for the study, wealth ranking was used as a basis for choosing farmers for interviewing. The services of a local field assistant of the farmer centre were available; he had the primary responsibility for wealth ranking. Four university students who were also native speakers were hired for two weeks to do the formal interviews. In the space of two weeks one village in each of 10 locations was chosen, the households

---

[6]Copies of this study 'Livestock Production in Lower Meru, and Implications for a Livestock Programme at Kamujine Farmers' Centre', by John Young, are available from the Intermediate Technology Development Group, Myson House, Railway Terrace, Rugby, CV21 3HT, UK.

wealth ranked, and a formal questionnaire administered to a sample of 129 farmers.

Background work

Using a map of the area, the approximate boundaries of the five AEZs were noted. The head of the centre (an area resident) and a few other local informants discussed the differences across and then within these zones. Together with the researcher they chose 10 locations in the centre's area. The locations were fairly large named areas, which included one or more villages. Reflecting the centre's interests, there was the following breakdown:

AEZ	Number of communities
1	1
2	3
3	3
4	2
5	1

In each agro-ecological zone, representative locations were chosen. In zones 2, 3 and 4, criteria for selection included access to roads/markets and length of settlement. A conscious effort was made to include a community with poor road access.

A discussion of about two hours with the university student enumerators was used to obtain background information on local words and the concepts of community, wealth, and household. The former posed some problems as in recent years communities based on clans (a broad kinship group) have given way to more socially heterogeneous communities. The Meru language includes several words meaning 'community'; one was chosen which refers to a purely spatial unit. Most households in the area are nuclear families: a man, wife and children. The household is named after the head, and is viewed as a single unit; the wealth of husband and wife together constitute the household wealth.

Location-level work during the formal study period

With the aid of the local sub-chiefs, meetings were held in each location to explain the purposes of the research. While other matters were discussed a few people were asked to help define the community boundaries, draw up the list of households and do the wealth ranking. This was done by the single field assistant. Within 12 days all 10 communities were covered. The university students administered the formal questionnaires to farmers chosen at random within each wealth rank.

Defining the community boundary and choosing a sub-area were the most difficult tasks. (In retrospect, it would have been preferable to do this before the day of the meeting.) In some locations there was only one village; in others there were up to six. The researcher and assistant first tried to get the name of each village within the named location. Then a brief description of how villages differed (e.g. near to town) was obtained. If possible, the villages themselves were wealth ranked. Then one village was chosen to represent the location. In the three locations of AEZ 3, the chosen villages were respectively described as (1) the most recently settled and poorest, (2) the richest, as many residents have shops in the nearby market, and (3) average, no real difference among villages so one was arbitrarily chosen. Thus, the sampling tried to cover a broad range of villages, using local informants' knowledge for selection.

Further difficulties arose as some villages were quite large (often numbering over 200 households). Further subdivision was then usually made on the basis of the clan of the household head. Members of the same clan tended

Wealth Ranking in Smallholder Communities

to live in the same part of the village. The names of each clan in the village were obtained and differences, if any, between clans in wealth were discussed. Then a representative clan was chosen. In one case a sub-group was chosen by using all of the households living in one part of the village. Specific footpaths were used to demarcate the area. These households were said to be representative of the community as a whole.

These same informants were used to elicit the names of all households in the selected sub-group. It was stressed that all households, including landless people and those with female heads, were to be included. This was done by mentally 'walking' the informants through the area and having them list the names of household heads. The number of households originally listed ranged from 30 to 174. The mean number of households ranked per chosen sub-group was 42.

Informant wealth ranking, grouping and sampling

The card sorting was done in the manner described earlier. In each of the 10 locations, three informants were used. Due to time constraints, it was not always possible for them to be from the village chosen. Occasionally, one or two informants from nearby areas were used. In one village, local officials, extension agents, were used instead of farmers. This was found to be unsatisfactory as their knowledge of individual households was limited. This practice is not recommended. The number of piles used ranged from three to eight, with a mean of five.

The researcher in charge of the study was particularly interested in the extremes of the wealth continuum. He reasoned that the very wealthy would have the most livestock. While the poor would have few livestock, the programme had a mandate to try to help them. He decided that three groups (rich, average, poor) would be sufficient, and as many as could be adequately handled in the short period available to him. Given his interest in wealth extremes he used cut-off points so that more farmers were put in the average rank than in either of the others. Overall, 22 per cent of the farmers were defined as rich, 45 per cent as average, and 33 per cent as poor.

Within each wealth category, the farmers to be interviewed were chosen opportunistically. An average of 13 farmers per village were interviewed, with approximately equal numbers per wealth category. Thus the sampling fraction was highest for the rich (46 per cent) lowest for the average group (24 per cent) and intermediate for the poor (29 per cent). This must be taken into account when data from farmers of the different wealth categories are combined to calculate village or area-wide averages. This problem could have been avoided by having initially made the groups more equal in size or by interviewing different numbers of farmers in each wealth group (i.e. three rich, six average, and four poor) to obtain a more equal sampling fraction.

It is impossible to verify the representativeness of the farmers interviewed for the whole area without conducting a comprehensive survey. However, the informants, field assistant, university enumerators and the researcher all believe the wealth ranking technique and associated sampling practices accurately distinguished households of very different wealth which is reflected in their land and livestock holdings and agricultural production practices. This was borne out by the formal survey. For example, in the areas of higher agricultural potential, local cattle were owned by 90 per cent of the rich, 50 per cent of average and no poor households. Of the households owning cross-bred dairy animals, 85 per cent were rich and 15 per cent were average. Whereas 70 per cent of the rich reported use of government sponsored veterinary services only 20 per cent of the poor did.

Much of the time devoted to the background work in Meru would have been required no matter how the feasibility study was conducted. The additional manpower required for wealth ranking was less than one man-day per community. Given the extreme importance of identifying wealth differences for understanding farmers' circumstances, production activities and training needs, it was clearly time well spent.

APPENDIX A

CHECKLIST FOR WEALTH RANKING

The following is a checklist of activities for wealth ranking for use in the field. It does not include overall background work. It is cross-referenced to pages of the manual.

A. General background activities (pp 11-12)
- discuss levels of 'community'; obtain words in local language
- discuss local concepts of wealth, decide on word or phrase
- define household in local language, obtain word or phrase.

B. Community specific background activities (pp 14-16)
- obtain names of all households; write on paper; verify and number them
- write name and number of each household on index card
- choose informant; explain basic nature of work
- find quiet place to interview, best with table.

C. Introduction to the informant (p 17)
Discuss:
- purpose of your research
- how rich different from poor generally in the area

- how problems of rich and poor are different
- chosen word for wealth in local language
- household concept; names on cards stand for whole household.

D. Actual card sorting (p 18)

- explain how it works; as many piles as he/she wants; can change number in course of it
- shuffle cards
- one by one, informant puts cards in piles
- review each pile to be sure cards in right one
- count piles to make sure no more than 40 per cent of farmers in any one. If there are, ask informant to subdivide
- write down household numbers by pile on a recording sheet (Figures 2-6)

E. Follow up discussion with informants (p 19)

- for each pile, ask informant what characterizes these farmers generally
- record responses by pile number
- ask informant how these farmers differ in terms of specific goals of the project.

F. Repeat C, D, E with two to three more informants

G. Compute average score and group (pp 33-37)

- write household numbers down in a line (Figure 7)
- write score for each household for each informant

$$\text{The score is:} \quad \frac{\text{Pile number of household} \times 100}{\text{Total number of piles}}$$

Note: Pile 1 is the richest.

- compute average scores for each household as total of its scores divided by the number of its scores
- household must have two scores to be included
- write average score for each household in large numbers on the index cards
- put index cards in order from lowest to highest average score (rich to poor)
- copy on a sheet of paper in this order: the position number, the average score and the household number (Figure 8)
- divide into 3 groups of near equal size.

APPENDIX B

SUGGESTED READING

The following are some suggested readings covering (A) FSR and background work on target areas; (B) some examples of the use of Wealth Ranking in different parts of the world; and (C) some case studies of the importance of wealth differences to smallholder farmers and pastoralists. Several overlapping references are given as these books and articles are not available everywhere.

A. FSR and background work on target areas

1. Shaner, W et al. (1982) *Farming Systems Research and Development: Guidelines for Developing Countries* (Westview Press: Boulder, Colorado).

A comprehensive overview and guide to all stages of farming systems research approach and methods. Includes information on FSR as it is practised by many different international agricultural research centres (IARCs).

2. 'Guidelines for agroforestry diagnosis and design' (Working Paper No 6); and 'Resources for agroforestry diagnosis and design' (Working Paper No 7) (ICRAF: Nairobi, Kenya).

WP 6 provides an overview of the FSR approach of ICRAF. WP 7 provides detailed step-by-step guidelines. Emphasis is on land use systems, rather than specific crops, making a good starting point for livestock researchers.

3. Byerlee, D et al. (1980) 'Planning Technologies Appropriate to Farmers: Concepts and Procedures' (CIMMYT: Mexico).

CIMMYT is the International Centre for the Improvement of Maize and Wheat. This early FSR manual emphasizes crop production but it is easy to use and much of its approach has wider relevance

4. Harrington, LW and Tripp, R (1984) 'Recommendation Domains: A Framework for On-farm Research'. CIMMYT Economics Programme Working Paper 02/84 (CIMMYT: Mexico).
   A detailed discussion of how to divide up a large target area into groups of farmers for whom the same agricultural recommendation would be suitable (called by CIMMYT a recommendation domain). Lists natural circumstances and socio-economic circumstances that might be important. The technique of wealth-ranking complements and expands on this approach.

5. 'Deriving Recommendation Domains for Central Province, Zambia', Report No 4 (CIMMYT Eastern Africa Economics Programme, Nairobi, Kenya).
   An excellent case study of the above (Reference No 4) including a sample questionnaire.

6. Hildebrand, PE (1981) 'Combining Disciplines in Rapid Appraisal: The Sondeo Approach', Agricultural Administration No 6 pp 423-432.
   An overview of ICTA's (International Centre for Tropical Agriculture) FSR approach.

7. Grosvenor-Alsop, Ruth. 'Wealth Ranking in a Caste Area in India'. ITDG (forthcoming 1988).

B. Wealth Differences: Some Examples

1. Grandin, BE (1983). 'The importance of Wealth in Pastoral Production. A rapid method for wealth ranking'.

Proceedings of workshop on pastoral systems research, ILCA, Addis Ababa, Ethiopia.

Part 1 presents some information on herd size differences in African pastoral systems and, for a Maasai area of Kenya, shows how many aspects of production correlate with wealth. Part 2 briefly reviews the wealth ranking technique

2. de Walt, B *Modernization in a Mexican Ejido,* Cambridge University Press, 1979.

Includes wealth ranking as part of an index of smallholder heterogeneity.

3. Grandin, BE (1980) 'Small cows, big money: wealth and dwarf cattle production in south-eastern Nigeria', PhD Thesis, Standford University. Available from University Microfilms, Ann Arbor, Michigan, USA or London, UK

4. Plattner, Stuart (1974) 'Wealth and growth among Mayan Indian peasants', *Human Ecology* 2: pp. 75-87.

A study in Mexico which used group interviews to obtain wealth ranks for a health and nutrition project

5. Sylvermann, S (1966). An ethnographic approach to social stratification: Prestige in a central Italian community. *American Anthropologist* 68: p. 899 ff.

Although based on 'prestige' rather than 'wealth', Sylvermann's work was the first to use local people to rank their neighbours.

C. Wealth Differences: Other Case Studies

1. Chambers, R (1983). *Rural development: putting the last first.* Longman, UK.

A strong, easy to read indictment of many current research and development activities which ignore or misunderstand poverty in rural areas. Excellent overview and bibliography.

2. Hill, P (1972). *Rural Hausa: A village and setting.* Cambridge University Press: Cambridge.

An overall study of inequality in a village and its agricultural production system which notes that 'there are many rich farmers who have entirely different economic aims from many poorer farmers'.

3. Cancian, F (1979) *The innovator's situation: upper middle class conservatism in agricultural communities.* Stanford University Press: Stanford, California.

Data from Western and non-Western systems shows wealth differences in attitudes towards innovation and risk.

4. Leonard, David K (1977) *Reaching the peasant farmer: organization theory and practice in Kenya* (University of Chicago Press: Chicago and London).

5. Dasgupta, Biplab (1975) 'A typology of village socio-economic systems from Indian village studies', *Economic and Political Weekly,* Volume 10 No 33, pp. 1394-1414.

6. Herren, Urs (1988) 'Pastoral Peasants: household strategies in Mukogodo Division, Lakipia District', IDS Working Paper No 458; Institute for Development Studies, University of Nairobi, Kenya.

Used Wealth Ranking for both sample selection and to obtain in-depth qualitative information on wealth differences in a number of communities.

www.ingramcontent.com/pod-product-compliance
Ingram Content Group UK Ltd.
Pitfield, Milton Keynes, MK11 3LW, UK
UKHW021831140426
5217IPUK00021B/1378